THE GREATEST
Cookery Tips
IN THE WORLD ®

by

Peter Osborne
'The Big Chef'

Illustrated by Graham Robson

Public Eye Publications

A Public Eye Publications Book

www.thegreatestintheworld.com

Illustrations:
Graham Robson, 'Drawing the Line'
info@dtline.co.uk

Cover design:
Setsquare Creative Design Consultants

Cover photo:
Clive Nichols
www.clivenichols.com

Layout design:
Bloomfield Ltd.

Copy editor:
Bronwyn Robertson
www.theartsva.com

Series creator / editor:
Steve Brookes

This first edition published in 2005 by
Public Eye Publications, PO Box 3182
Stratford-upon-Avon, Warwickshire CV37 7XW

A CIP catalogue record for this book is available from the British Library
ISBN 1-905151-04-7

Printed and bound by Ashford Colour Press limited, Gosport, Hampshire PO13 0FW

I would like to dedicate this book to my family.

First of all to my Dad, sadly no longer with
us, who never saw this part of my life
but has inspired me in so many ways.
Hope you are watching, Dad!

Then to the four women in my life. My Mum,
who watches and listens to every show;
my lovely wife Anna-Marie; our beautiful
daughter Amelia and not forgetting our cat,
Puss Puss, who is probably the best
fed cat in the neighbourhood!

Thank you all for your love, help and
support over the years.

I would also like to thank Christine for taking
time out of her busy life to write
the foreword to this book. She really is a
remarkable lady and a lovely friend.

I hope you all enjoy the book!

Contents

A few words from Christine Hamilton...

Peter Osborne burst into my life when I interviewed him at 'The Ideal Home Show' for a radio show which Neil and I were presenting. He steamed into the studio looking like a large exotic, fruit meringue on legs wearing a white chef's jacket and multi-coloured trousers. It was immediately obvious he is devoted not only to cooking but also to eating! I entirely endorse Peter's maxim: "Never trust a thin chef". If portion size, in the person of the chef, is any guide to culinary ability, then Peter is exceptionally well-endowed!

During our interview (and, indeed, ever since) I have profited from Peter's wealth of hints and tips gathered over many years. He is always willing to share his expertise, in a witty yet easily-understood way, with TV viewers, radio listeners and audiences at his live shows. In fact with anyone who will listen and let's be honest – he loves talking!

When Granada TV asked Neil and me to take over a restaurant for a day and cook for some unsuspecting punters, my instinctive reaction was to ring Peter for advice. Cooking against the clock with inadequate facilities (well, Neil can hardly boil water without expert help!) needed every ounce of Peter's wit and wisdom. He surpassed himself and, with his help, so did we.

At last, Peter has whipped up his best tips into a gourmet confection and here they are for your delectation. Good cooks are not necessarily able to impart their expertise. Peter's advice is simple but practical and I promise you there is no 'gobbledy-cook'. Not only will his tips make your life and your cooking easier, they will save you time and money as well.

However clever you may be, however accomplished in the kitchen, you cannot live without this book!

Christine
X

The Greatest Cookery Tips In The World

Fresh eggs

To check the freshness of an egg, dissolve 2 tablespoons (30ml) of salt in about 1 pint (268ml) of water. Place the egg in the water. If the egg sinks then it is fresh, if it floats then it is stale.

Perky mash

To revive lifeless mashed potatoes, just whisk an egg
white until stiff and fold carefully into the potatoes. Put the
mixture into a dish and bake in a hot oven until fluffy and
golden.

Peeling hard boiled eggs

The shells of hard-boiled eggs are easy to remove if done
so while the eggs are still slightly warm from cooking.
Refrigerating them with the shells on tends to bind the
outer covering to the cooked egg. Briefly cool the eggs
in running water after cooking. Peel, cover and store them
in the refrigerator until needed. They should keep well for
two to three days.

Sharpening mug!

If you don't have a steel to sharpen your knives use the
base of an unglazed earthenware mug. Run the blade
across it at a slight angle. Do this several times in the
same direction and then turn over to do the other side.

Egg temperature

Eggs should be brought to room temperature before use,
so if you do keep them in the refrigerator, try to remember
to take them out an hour before using.

Kitchen safety

- Whilst cooking can be satisfying and enjoyable, it can also be disastrous if safety is not observed. Whilst the following tips for kitchen safety may appear obvious, it can be so easy to forget for a moment, especially when children are helping out...

- Avoid leaving food that is cooking unattended for a long period of time, if at all. If using a timer, have it with you at all times to remind you that you have something cooking in the kitchen.

- Turn handles of pots and pans inward and not sticking out.

- Avoid reaching over the stovetop when cooking and watch your sleeves – especially over a gas hob.

- Keep curtains, potholders, towels, and any other combustibles away from cooking areas.

- Do not put knives or other sharp objects into a full sink. Someone could reach in and accidentally get hurt.

- Never store sharp knives in drawers with other kitchen utensils. It is too easy to forget they are there when searching for something in a hurry.

- Never attempt to catch a falling knife. Let it fall.

- When processing hot liquids in a blender (such as sauces and soups), make sure the blender's lid is back on, then cover the lid with a towel and your hand, before proceeding to blend. Also, do not fill the blender more than halfway.

Continued over the page......

Kitchen Safty continued.....

- Keep children and pets away from appliances when cooking.

- Wash your dishcloths, towels and sponges frequently to get rid of bacteria or simply replace them more often.

- Keep appliance cords as short as possible to avoid accidents such as tripping or knocking the appliance over.

- Have a small fire extinguisher and a first aid kit readily accessible in the kitchen. Also make sure that smoke detectors are fitted throughout your house – not just one at the bottom of the stairs.

Juicy citrus

Citrus fruits such as lemons and oranges, should feel heavy for their size if they are full of juice. They will also yield most juice if they are stored at room temperature. If they have been stored in a fridge, microwave each one for about 4 seconds to increase the amount of juice produced.

Filling without a funnel

To fill jars without spills, if you don't have a funnel, improvise by using a washing up liquid bottle. Remove the lid and cut off the base of the bottle. Wash and dry thoroughly before use.

Get the best from herbs

Get the most out of fresh herbs by adding them to a recipe at the ideal time. The flavour of tough-leaved herbs like rosemary, thyme or sage benefit from long cooking times. Add these herbs near the beginning of a preparation. The more delicate varieties such as basil, parsley and tarragon respond best to short simmering. Add them near the end of the recipe.

Peeling tomatoes

Recipes sometimes call for peeled fresh tomatoes. This can easily be done by dropping the whole tomato in boiling water for five seconds. Carefully remove the tomato and then drop immediately into cold water. The skin should then be split, making it easy to peel off.

Sweat-free cheese

When you buy cheese wrapped in plastic, remove the wrapping as soon as you get home. Then wrap the cheese tightly in greaseproof paper, this will stop it from sweating and it will keep for longer.

Freezing bananas

Banana skins become flecked when ripe and it's best to eat the fruit at this stage. If you are worried about bananas becoming over-ripe or if you find yourself with an over-abundance, try freezing them for later cooking uses. Wrapped in cling film, still in their skins, they will keep in the freezer for up to six months. Eat them while still slightly frozen, or mash them and use in drinks or baking. Don't worry if the peel darkens during freezing as the fruit inside will still be pale. As with most foods, freezing changes the texture of bananas so they are best used in recipes like breads, pies, puddings, cakes, and ice cream. Use them within four to six months of freezing.

Soften hard sugar

If you have a dish or bag of hardened brown sugar, place a slice of apple in it to soften it again.

Ripe melons

To check the ripeness of a melon, hold it firmly in both hands and lightly press around the end of the melon, opposite the stem. The surface should give slightly under the pressure. A ripe melon will also have a pleasant sweet smell.

Cutting for success

Cutting foods into a uniform size and shape may be important to the visual presentation of dishes but it is perhaps more important to the success of the recipe as it allows the ingredients to cook at the same rate. If you add some carrots to a soup that are 1/4 inch (6mm) thick and some that are 1 inch (25mm) thick you can expect an uneven result as one will either be overcooked or undercooked.

Easy-peel shallots

Shallots are peeled more easily when you pour boiling water over them, leave for 30 seconds then drain.

Ripening tomatoes

Tomatoes that are picked or purchased before they are ripe can be made ready for use in your kitchen. Contrary to popular belief, sunlight does not ripen a picked tomato (it will cause it to firm up, not truly ripen). Gentle heat will cause the tomatoes to ripen. Place them in a warm area of your kitchen (near your stove) and check them often.

To ripen tomatoes quickly, place them in a paper bag with an apple. Leave in a cool dark place and the tomatoes will ripen in a couple of days. As the apple ripens, it gives off a gas called ethylene which speeds up the ripening of the tomatoes. A banana will do a similar job but the strong smell may taint the tomato.

Butter frying

When frying with butter, prevent it from burning by adding a little cooking oil as it melts.

Reviving a French loaf

To revive a stale French loaf, cut it into thick slices almost to the base then spread garlic butter between the slices. Wrap in foil, and bake in a hot oven for 10 minutes.

Grilling in an oven

When grilling in an oven always leave the oven door open. If the door remains closed the air cannot circulate and you end up baking the food rather than grilling it!

Food glazing

Brushing foods with products like marmalades or jellies is a simple way to add flavour during the last few minutes of broiling. Chicken and pork are especially good when paired with fruit glazes. Chicken goes well with apricot jelly or lemon marmalade and try pork with redcurrant jelly, Jalapeño jelly or orange marmalade. Preserves and maple syrup can also help create interesting new flavours. Remember that all these products have high sugar content and can quickly burn.

Size your vegetables

When buying vegetables such as Brussels sprouts try to choose all the same size so that they all cook at an even rate. If you are hosting an important dinner party similar sized vegetables look much nicer on the plate!

Non-slip worktop

To stop a chopping board or bowl from moving on a kitchen worktop during use, place a damp tea-towel underneath first.

Buying chillies

When you are purchasing varieties of hot chillies you are not familiar with, as a general rule of thumb, the smaller the size of the chilli, the hotter the flavour will be.

Sprouting potatoes

To prevent potatoes from sprouting when stored, place an apple amongst them.

Roasting garlic

Roasted garlic adds a rich full flavour to dressings, sauces, and marinades and can be prepared easily at home. The supermarket bought varieties tend to have lost a lot of their flavour by the time they are purchased so try home-grown cloves or those bought from independent greengrocers. Pre-heat your oven to 325°F/150°C/gas mark 4. Toss about ten cloves (skins on) with two tablespoons of olive oil. Place in a roasting pan, sprinkle on a little water and season with salt and pepper. Place on a baking tray, loosely cover with foil and cook for about 45 minutes. Cool slightly and squeeze the garlic from its skin into a small bowl. If not using immediately, place in a covered container and refrigerate until needed.

Frozen wine cubes

Never throw away any unused wine left after parties. It can
be easily frozen in ice cube trays and then dropped into
soups and sauces as required.

Richer pot roast

A simple way to enrich the gravy for a pot roast is to make
a rich roux. Melt 2 tablespoons of butter in a saucepan,
whisk in 4 tablespoons of flour and cook for 5 minutes,
stirring frequently. Set this aside. After your roast has been
cooking for 3/4 of its designated cooking time, carefully
drain off all but 1 cup of the liquid from the roasting dish
into the saucepan with the flour and butter mix. Cook for
5 minutes, stirring often. Pour the mixture over the roast,
cover and complete the cooking time.

The cooked cake test

A cocktail stick or toothpick can be used to test whether a
cake is ready; if it comes out clean then the cake is ready.

Sugar substitute

Add a much richer flavour in baking recipes by substituting
honey or golden syrup for granulated sugar. For 4oz
(100g) of sugar simply replace with 7oz (200g) of honey.
Remember that honey and syrup contain about 20% water
so you may need to reduce the liquid content of some
recipes accordingly. Try using half honey and half sugar in
bread recipes.

Sticky lids

Before resealing a jar or bottle of sticky food, wipe the rim
and lid with a paper towel that has been dampened with
hot water; this will prevent the lid from getting sticky.

Cool pastry

To keep your pastry cool and easy to handle, instead of using a rolling pin use a straight sided, corked wine bottle and fill with chilled water. Chill in the bottle first if necessary.

Lighter scrambled egg

Add a small amount of water to your eggs before whipping them for scrambling. This produces steam during cooking and makes for a lighter finished product. Avoid adding milk, as it tends to make the eggs tough.

Add flavour to your barbeque

A great way to add flavour when barbequing meats and vegetables is to smoke with fresh herbs. Choose medium-sized bunches of rosemary or thyme and soak them in water for at least 15 minutes. Shake off the excess water and place them directly on the hot coals. Replace the grill and add the food immediately. This method works really well with pork, chicken, or lamb.

Storing an iced cake

Store an iced cake on the lid of a cake tin, with the inverted tin over it. You can then slice and remove pieces without risking damage trying to take the cake out of the tin.

Storing vegetables

Take potatoes, carrots etc. out of the supermarket plastic bags as soon as you get home. This will stop them sweating and they will stay fresh for longer.

Boiling eggs

When boiling eggs, prevent the shells from cracking by adding a pinch of salt to the water first. If eggshells do crack during boiling add a little vinegar to the water. This will set the white and prevent any further egg white or yolk from leaking out.

To prevent black rings from forming around the yolks of hard-boiled eggs, drain them as soon as they are cooked and crack the shells under cold running water to cool quickly.

No caster sugar?

To make caster sugar from granulated sugar, place the granulated sugar into a food processor with a metal blade and whiz for a few seconds to get the right consistency.

Chilli too hot?

If you have made Chilli con Carne that is too hot and spicy, add a dollop of mayonnaise and stir in well. This will cool down the dish.

Choosing a coconut

Canned coconut milk works nicely enough for most recipes, but there is nothing like the taste of the milk fresh from the nut. When choosing one, look for a coconut that is heavy for its size. You should be able to hear the liquid sloshing around when you shake it; if you don't, the coconut has dried out.

Drying herbs

When drying herbs use the clean bags provided with the tablets for washing machines. Put in the fresh herbs and hang them to dry. When they are ready just rub the bags between your hands onto a piece of paper and then store the dried herbs that fall out of them in empty jars. All the herb stems will be left in the bags making it a very quick and easy method.

Rescuing over-salted cooking

Over-salted vegetables, casseroles or other dishes can
be saved by dropping a peeled, cut potato into the water.
Simmer until the potato is soft then carefully lift it out. The
potato should have absorbed a lot of the saltiness. Other
ways to disguise saltiness are by adding a small can of
tomatoes, a dash of sweet sherry or a little plain yoghurt,
whichever is most suitable for the particular dish involved.

Keep an eye on mussels

Discard any mussels that have shells which are open before cooking or closed after cooking.

Flavoursome gravy

Use the vegetable water from boiled vegetables when making gravy. This way you get more flavour and won't waste the goodness that has come out of the vegetables into the water.

The wonder of bay

Bay leaves are an indispensable ingredient in the kitchen and add flavour to many soups, stocks and stews. They are the basis of the French 'bouquet garni'. This is a mixture of bay and several additional herbs tied together in cheesecloth, then dropped into a simmering pot. Bay leaves are especially good as flavourings for various savoury, carbohydrate dishes such as potato casseroles, bean stews and risotto. Most modern recipes suggest that the bay leaf is removed before serving the dish, as it can potentially cause someone to choke. Always use the leaves sparingly or they will make a dish too bitter.

In the past many traditions grew up around the fate of the person who found a bay leaf in their bowl. Many families rewarded the finder with extra dessert. Some believed that the person was entitled to a wish. However, others assigned the task of washing the dishes or clearing the table to the recipient of the bay leaf!

Longer-lasting fruit cake

To improve the life of a large fruit cake cut it in half, take slices from the middle of the cake and then slide the two halves back together. Store the cake in an airtight container.

Refreshed fish

Thawed fish can still retain a stale 'frozen' taste. By thawing in milk the taste is replaced by a 'freshly caught' flavour.

Garlic oil

Garlic that cooks to the point of browning can add a bitter taste to a dish. Always add the garlic to hot oil near the end of the cooking process. An alternative method is to cook with garlic-infused oil. Simply warm the oil over medium heat, remove from the flame and add the fresh chopped garlic. Allow to steep. Strain and use when preparing recipes calling for garlic. Use about 1 teaspoon (5ml) of garlic to 1/4 pint (150ml) of water.

Freezing cheese

Only freeze cheese containing more than 45% fat. Cheese with a lower fat content will separate and become grainy when frozen. Previously frozen cheeses are best used in cooking (sauces, pizzas, casseroles, etc.). Hard grating cheese (Parmesan, Romano as well as semi soft varieties like Swiss, Cheddar, and Mozzarella) can be more successfully frozen than soft cheeses (Brie, Camembert).

Useful dried herbs and spices

Keeping your herbs and spices cabinet well stocked is the key to easier cooking and baking. In addition to salt and black pepper, the following should always be in your cupboard:

Dried Basil	Garlic Powder
Dried Parsley	Chilli Powder
Ground Cinnamon	Dill
Ground Ginger	Dried Oregano
Paprika	Dried Rosemary
Dried Thyme	Vanilla Extract

Slicing apples

Apples tend to brown very quickly after being diced or sliced. Add 2 teaspoons (10ml) of lemon juice to a bowl of water and place the cut apples in the lemon water until served or added to a recipe. The apples will keep their colour and texture perfectly.

Frying technique

A simple technique can help prevent breaded or battered foods from sticking when preparing them in a basket-type fryer. When the oil has reached the desired temperature, hold the food item with tongs away from the sides and bottom of the pan and partially submerge it in the oil for 10 seconds before releasing it to cook. This sets the coating and makes it less likely to adhere to the fryer's basket.

Over-spiced dish?

If you've overdone the spices in a dish, a bit of sugar will balance it out. Lemon juice also helps so put in half a lemon, cook for a few minutes then remove.

Stain removal

Amazingly a potato will take food stains off your fingers. Just slice and rub the raw potato on the stains and then rinse with water.

Burnt rice

If you burn a pot of rice, place a slice of white bread on the top of the rice. Let it sit for a few minutes. The burnt taste will adsorbed into the bread and the rice will taste fine. Be sure not to scrape the bottom of the pan when serving.

Smooth running salt cellar

To avoid your salt cellar clogging up, put a few grains of rice in with the salt, this will absorb the moisture which causes the salt to stick together and the cellar to clog.

Bread revival

A slightly stale loaf of bread can be perked up by placing it in a colander over a saucepan of boiling water. Cover with the pan lid until the bread is warm.

Flour shaker

To make a home made flour shaker, make several holes
in the metal lid of a screw top jar by hammering a nail
through it while resting it on a wooden board. Fill the jar
with flour and replace the lid.

Wait before salting meat

Never salt meat before cooking as it will draw out all the juices and toughen the meat.

Does that knife need sharpening?

Every kitchen should have a good sharpening steel as part of the knife set. The main misconception, however, is that a steel actually sharpens the knife – it doesn't! The purpose of the steel is to finely tune the edge of a knife by removing the metal burrs caused by normal use. This is done every time the knife appears 'dull'. When the knife needs to be sharpened again, this must be done using a proper sharpening stone and oil or carried out professionally. Good quality knives will last must longer if they are looked after in this way.

Easy-peel hard boiled eggs

A few simple tips can make peeling hard-boiled eggs easy. Add the fresh eggs to a saucepan of cold water containing 1 teaspoon of salt. Bring to a boil, cover and remove from the heat. Allow the eggs to sit in the water for about 15 minutes. Drain off the warm water and place the eggs in iced water. Allow to chill thoroughly before peeling.

Shopping list

Always keep a current shopping list on view in the kitchen
– maybe attached to the refrigerator door with a magnet.
Each time you use up an item of food, add it to the list.
When you go shopping, take a bulldog clip or clothes peg
with you to attach your shopping list to the trolley so that it
doesn't get lost.

Salted or unsalted butter?

Are there any advantages to using unsalted butter? Some cooks believe it is better to add salt to a dish as needed rather than to be locked in on the salt content of an ingredient. Salt can also mask the off flavour of butter that isn't at its freshest point. Because dessert recipes use very little salt, using unsalted butter can definitely help assure the desired end result.

Fresher packed lunches

To keep packed lunches fresh and at a safe temperature, freeze a part of the lunch, e.g. a small tub of yoghurt or a carton of fruit juice. Pop this into an insulated lunch bag and it will keep the rest of the food nicely chilled until lunchtime.

Non-stick cheese

To keep cheese from sticking to the grater first spray the grater with non-stick cooking spray – it works a treat!

Non-stick honey

To measure honey and syrups easily, use a metal spoon that has been dipped in hot water. Honey and syrups will not stick to the heated spoon.

Storing eggs

It is best to store eggs in the refrigerator as this slows down the aging and therefore they will keep longer. Store them in a carton to prevent them from losing moisture and being tainted by nearby strong flavoured food. Always store eggs with the pointed end down as this keeps the yolk in the centre and helps to keep the egg fresh.

Perfect melted chocolate

Following a few simple guidelines can help ensure success when melting chocolate for a recipe. First make sure that the bowl (stainless steel or glass) is totally dry and add the chocolate to the bowl in small pieces. Always place the bowl over steaming, not boiling water.

A microwave oven also works well for melting chocolate. Place the chocolate pieces in a microwaveable dish. Set the oven on medium power (50%) and heat for 40 seconds for 1oz (28g), 1 minute for 2oz (57g), 2 minutes for 4oz (113g) and 3 minutes for 8oz (226g). Stop the oven and stir once halfway through the melting process.

Freezing stock

If you have any flavoursome, unused stock left over after cooking then don't waste it. It can be stored easily by freezing in ice cube trays and keeping in a plastic bag in the freezer.

Keep a check on herbs and spices

It is reasonably obvious to say that dried herbs and spices will not last forever! For the best flavour they should be used within two years of packaging. Usage after this time is safe, but some loss of flavour may be noticeable. Proper storage of spices will ensure maximum flavour and colour retention. Heat, light and moisture are all enemies of dried spices. Heat causes flavour loss, light will fade the naturally bright colours, and moisture can cake ground and powdered spices. Keep spices in a cool, dry, and dark cupboard away from the cooker or any source of intense heat.

It is best to open and visually check spices and herbs annually. Crush a small amount of the spice or herb in your hand and smell it. If the aroma is not rich, full and immediate, the spice or herb has probably lost much of its potency. The exceptions are whole spices such as peppercorns and cinnamon sticks. These have a protective outer coating and will not release their full fragrance until broken or crushed.

Continued over the page . . .

47

Keep a check on herbs and spices continued.....

Compare the aroma of a freshly purchased spice or herb
to that which you've stored for a year or more to see
the difference. Be aware, however, that subtle changes
may also occur with each new crop of herb or spice.
Green, leafy herbs will fade upon aging but different
herbs naturally vary in colour and should not always be
compared with each other. Tarragon, for example, is
naturally greener in colour than rosemary. Also some dill
products contain the flower portion, giving them a more
yellow colour than those without the inclusion of flowers.
Red coloured spices, such as paprika, red pepper and
chilli powder, will turn from red to brown in colour with age,
however they may still be perfectly okay to use.

Spices and herbs are made up of numerous flavour
components. Each component dissipates at varying rates,
altering the overall balance of flavours as they age. The
initial quality of a spice and herb can have an impact on
its shelf life, with a high quality product retaining its good
flavour longer than a lower quality version.

Simple cake decoration

A fast and effective way to finish a cake requires only
a paper lace-type doily and powdered sugar (or cocoa
powder). Simply centre the doily on top of the cake and
sprinkle on a light, even layer of icing sugar or cocoa.
Carefully lift the doily off the cake (straight up) and you
should be left with an attractive design.

Oven temperature

Check the accuracy of your oven temperature by placing
an oven thermometer in the centre of the oven. Heat to
200°C/400°F/gas mark 6 and compare. If there is a large
discrepancy then in future adjust the cooking temperature
accordingly or, better still, call in an engineer to replace the
thermostat.

Heating cream

If you want to heat cream for a recipe then use double
cream which does not separate as easily as single or
soured cream. Alternatively you can substitute crème
fraiche.

Cutting in

You may come across the term 'cut in' when preparing
certain baking recipes. This means to combine a dry
ingredient (like flour) with a solid fat (usually butter or
margarine). The end result should be small, crumb-like
particles. This can be done easily by using the pulse
feature of a food processor. Other methods include
working the ingredients between two knives or gently
kneading them with your fingers.

Grape tips

Before buying grapes you should shake the bunch gently, if grapes fall off the bunch is not fresh. To store grapes, wrap loosely in newspaper and keep in the dark.

Freezing tomatoes

If you find yourself with an abundance of tomatoes from your garden at the end of the growing season (or great prices at the farmers' market or 'pick your own') try freezing them. They will not be suitable for slicing, but their flavour will be better than canned tomatoes when used in soups, stews or sauces. Remove the stems and, after rinsing and drying, place them whole in a plastic freezer bag. You can also chop them and puree them in a food processor before freezing the thick liquid. Add some fresh chopped basil to a few of the bags for ready to cook Italian-style sauce bases.

When you need whole tomatoes for cooking simply run a frozen one under the tap for a few seconds and slide off the skin. They can be sliced while frozen and are also quick and easy to deseed when half thawed. Remember that, once frozen, tomatoes can only be used for cooking purposes; they are not suitable for salads.

An alternative way to freeze tomatoes is to remove the stem top, cut the tomatoes in half and place, cut side up, in a roasting pan. Drizzle them with a little oil. Roast uncovered at 150°C/300°F/gas mark 6 for 2 hours. Allow them to cool, place in plastic bags and freeze. They will be great in winter soups, stews, casseroles, pasta sauces and chilli.

Crispy jackets

When cooking jacket potatoes in the microwave, the skins will be much crispier if you rub salt into them first.

Cooking spinach

To cook spinach quickly and retain its quality, buy it in the sealed plastic bags from the supermarket, make a couple of holes in the top and cook in a microwave on high for 90 seconds. Open the bag and serve immediately. Quick cooking like this means that the days of soggy spinach have gone!

Preserving with lemon juice

Most cooks know that to keep an avocado looking good you squeeze lemon or lime juice over it as soon as you expose its flesh to air. However lemon juice also prevents peaches, bananas, apples, and pears from turning brown, as well as bringing out their best flavours.

Extra virgin olive oil

Olive oils labelled 'extra virgin' must have an acidity level below 1%. They usually come from the first pressing of the olives. A good extra virgin olive oil should be used as a condiment and never used for cooking. The fruity flavour is somewhat subtle. Sprinkle it over bread, fresh Mozzarella or salad greens.

The perfect cup of coffee

If you make your coffee with tap water, let the water run for a while to add extra oxygen. This will give your coffee a much fuller-bodied flavour. To make the perfect cup of coffee, like the ones you buy in the best coffee bars, always use 2 tablespoons of ground coffee per 6 fl.oz (175ml) of water.

Roasting on a rack

Roasting meats on a rack can be beneficial in two ways. First it allows excess fat to drip off and not be included in the final dish. It also lets the heat circulate completely around the meat, which makes for even cooking. It is especially useful for items like poultry or a leg of lamb.

Keeping butter

Unsalted butter will keep in a freezer for six months, but salted butter will successfully freeze for only three months.

Feta cheese

Cubes of feta cheese can be stored in a jar of olive oil with sprigs of herbs or garlic cloves added for flavour, if desired. The wonderfully flavoured oil can be used later for salad dressings.

Cooking fish

Selecting the best way to prepare particular varieties of fish can help ensure the success of a meal. Basically, most fish fall into two categories: fatty and lean. Fatty fish include trout, tuna, salmon, and swordfish. These types benefit from 'dry' cooking methods like grilling, baking, or broiling. The lean fish include cod, sole, and bass. They are best cooked using a 'wet' method like steaming, frying, or poaching. Ask your fishmonger about the fat content of a particular variety.

Get the defrosting bug!

Get into the habit of defrosting the refrigerator and freezer regularly, unless they do this automatically or are 'frost-free'. This helps to make sure that they are working properly and efficiently, so that the food inside is stored correctly and safely.

Snacks in a hurry

Making quick snacks or light meals is easy if you keep a few items in the cupboard. The formula is bread item + cheese + sauce + meat (optional). An example would be tortillas + cheddar + salsa + beef = burrito. Remember that the bread items usually freeze well.

Try different combinations of the following to create new dishes...

1) Muffins
2) Pita
3) Cheeses (like Cheddar and Mozzarella)
4) Salsa
5) Minced beef (browned and frozen)
6) Italian pasta sauce (jar)
7) Cooked frozen diced chicken
8) Tortillas
9) Tinned meat (ham, corned beef etc.)
10) Onions

Buying cauliflowers

When buying cauliflowers always pull back the leaves to make sure the florets are white all the way around the head.

Ice cubes

To store ice cubes for a party remove from the ice trays and place on a baking sheet in the freezer for a couple of hours. You can then store them in a bag without them sticking together.

What does scoring mean?

Whilst I am sure that all your meals will get 10 out of 10, the technique of scoring involves making shallow cuts into foods before cooking! This is done for several reasons. It can allow a marinade to enter and therefore flavour meats more easily, help cuts of beef flatten out and thus cook evenly, or it is sometimes used to tenderise foods. The thickest parts of a fish are often scored to assure even cooking. Ham is often cut in this way to create a decorative design.

Pasta or noodles?

The main difference between pastas and noodles is that most noodles contain egg (or egg yolks) and most pasta does not. There are exceptions to this rule. Some recipes for making fresh pasta call for egg to be added. There are also 'no-yolk' noodles available! People on restricted diets may wish to check the listed ingredients before choosing which product to purchase.

Instant thickening

Instant potato powder or granules are excellent for thickening gravy, soups etc. as they won't make lumps like flour often does.

White or brown rice?

There are a few facts you may wish to consider when choosing rice for a recipe. Brown rice (whole grain with only the husk removed) is higher in fibre and more nutritious. It has a nutty flavour and chewy texture that may not be suitable for some preparations. Brown rice also takes longer to cook. Processed white rice has a neutral flavour and tends to take on the flavours of the ingredients it is prepared with. Choose the right rice product for the desired end result.

Wrapping butter

Always wrap butter well before you store it in the fridge as it easily picks up odours from any strong foods kept near it. Alternatively, if your fridge has special lidded compartments in the door, then always keep your butter in one of these.

Freezing cream

Open freeze double cream in an ice cube tray, then turn
out the cubes into polythene bags for storing in the freezer.
The frozen cream cubes can be added straight into hot
soups, sauces or casseroles.

Overcooked vegetables

If you overcook carrots, peas, parsnips or swede then
drain well, place in a food processor and puree until
smooth. Add a little cream to taste and, hey presto, you
have a rich creamy vegetable puree!

Weekly refrigerator check

It's a good idea to make a weekly 'quality check' of the
contents of your refrigerator. This can save you a lot of
money. Always check the freshness of your vegetables.
If they are starting to fade it might be a good time to make
soup! Leftover meats should also be examined and
disposed of if they are over their recommended fridge
storage times.

No more bubbling jam

To stop jam bubbling out of jam tarts before the pastry is cooked, keep the jam in the fridge before use – simple but very effective.

Wooden skewers

Grilling foods on skewers makes for great presentation. Following a few guidelines can help ensure success. Be sure to soak wooden skewers in water for about 20 minutes before pushing on the food, and wrap the exposed 'handle' end with aluminium foil. Both of these techniques will help prevent the wood burning. To prevent over or under-cooking of individual items, partially cook long-cooking foods (like peppers and onions) before placing them on skewers with fast-cooking items such as chicken, mushrooms and cherry tomatoes.

Dried mushrooms

To revive mushrooms that have dried out, add a little red wine and leave to soak for a few minutes. Then bring to the boil, stir in a little cream and chopped parsley and serve.

Keeping bread fresh

If you don't have a bread bin or crock, keep bread fresh by using a clean, dry tea towel or a cotton drawstring bag. Wash and dry the bag regularly to prevent mould from developing. A loaf can also be kept on a wooden breadboard and covered with an upturned earthenware bowl.

Marinating

Marinades for barbecues can be created easily by remembering that they are made by using three basic food types:

Oil: Any type from corn oil to olive oil.
Acid: This could be wine, fruit juice, or vinegar.
Seasonings: Herbs and spices to suit the food you are preparing.

Experiment with different combinations to create your own scrumptious summer recipes.

Freezing dough

If you make your own bread, any leftover un-risen dough can be wrapped up well and frozen for about a month.

Freezing a gateau

When freezing a large cake or gateau, cut it into slices before freezing, and interleave each slice with a piece of non-stick greaseproof paper. Reassemble the cake and freeze as usual. You can then remove as many slices as you need without having to thaw the whole cake.

Fresh beans

To check the freshness of a runner bean, hold it between
your forefinger and thumb and bend it gently. If it is fresh it
will break in two rather than bend.

Safe knife storage

A safe way to store sharp kitchen knives is in a slot cut into the back of a worktop behind a drawer unit. The blades are then hidden behind the drawer and out of the way of small children.

Saving energy

If you have solid electric rings, then save energy by turning them off a few minutes before you finish cooking. The food will continue to cook on the remaining heat.

Freshly ground pepper

Many cooks would consider a pepper mill more of a necessity than a gadget. The taste of freshly-ground pepper over pre-ground can be compared with the difference between fresh herbs and the dried varieties. Keep one mill in the kitchen for cooking and one on the table for seasoning.

Safe cutting

- Prevent injuries while slicing and dicing by following a few simple tips...

- Always place a damp towel under the cutting board to limit movement.

- Be sure to get a 'flat side down' before preparing round items like onions or lemons. This can be done by cutting them down the middle and placing the flat side on the board before chopping.

- Always wash, bleach and rinse the board after each use, especially when cutting meat, poultry or seafood. If possible, have separate boards for fresh meats, cooked meats and vegetables.

Blanching

Recipes sometimes call for a technique called blanching or parboiling. This is the process whereby the item is quickly cooked (usually in boiling water) for a brief period of time. The food is usually refreshed afterwards in cold water to stop the cooking. This method is often used in preparing fresh vegetables for freezing.

Fresh corn

Fresh corn kernels (as opposed to canned or frozen) can add flavour to most recipes. Corn can easily be removed form the cob by following a few simple tips. After removing the husk and silk, stand the ear on its end on a cutting board. Hold the corn using a clean dishtowel and carefully run a sharp knife down the ear, pressing the knife against the cob at a slight angle to remove the kernels.

Burnt hob

Try this to remove food burnt around a solid hob: once the hob has cooled, place a kitchen cloth in a solution of washing up liquid and water, wring it out and place onto the hob. Leave for two hours and then wipe clean.

Easy slicing of dried fruit

In recipes calling for dates, apricots or prunes, you will find the dried fruit easier to work with, especially to slice, if you chill it first in the refrigerator or even the freezer. The colder the fruit is, the easier it is to chop or slice.

Homemade mini icing bags

To make small icing bags, take a freezer bag and place the icing inside. Close the bag and snip a small hole in one corner. It is essential to use freezer quality bags as the sandwich ones are not strong enough and will burst when you try to squeeze out the icing.

Adding fruit to batter

If you're adding dried fruit to a cake or bread batter, coat the pieces of fruit with flour before adding to the mix. This will keep the fruit from dropping through the batter and appearing at the bottom of the cake or loaf.

Storing vegetable oils

All vegetable oils should be stored in a cool, dark cabinet to protect them from light, heat, and air. When exposed to air, fatty acids become rancid, which means they combine with oxygen to form hydro peroxides, natural substances that taste bad, smell bad, and even destroy the oh-so-good-for-you vitamin E in the oil.

Cleaning chrome trim

To clean rust from chrome trim in the kitchen, rub it with a piece of aluminium foil, shiny side out, then buff with a soft cloth.

Bacteria-free sponges

To disinfect and kill bacteria in kitchen sponges, (the cleaning variety – not the cake!), wash the sponge thoroughly, and then microwave it, while it is wet, for approx. 30 to 40 seconds on high. Watch carefully and when you see steam from the sponge, the bacteria in the sponge will be dead and you can stop the microwave. Remove the sponge carefully as it will be very hot! When cool, wash the sponge thoroughly before use. Never use this tip with a sponge that has any metal components.

Simple classy garnish

You can create a simple and colourful garnish for most dishes using bell peppers. Purchase one each of the green, red and yellow varieties. Split them lengthwise. Remove the seeds and membranes and cut them into 2-inch strips. Place the "shiny" side down on a cutting board. Carefully slice off the inner part (using a horizontal motion) leaving only brightly coloured outer skin. Dice into tiny (1/16 of an inch) squares. Sprinkle on foods or on the rim of the plate.

Microwaving wedges

When cooking wedge shaped items in a microwave, point the narrow side towards the middle of the microwave and the item will cook more evenly.

Protect non-stick pans

To protect the non-stick linings of pans when stacked together, place a sheet of kitchen paper between each pan before storing.

Fat-free stock

This simple recipe makes about 1 litre of a flavourful, fat-free stock to add to soups and sauces...

2 medium onions
3 medium carrots
3 sticks celery
1 handful parsley with stems
3 cloves garlic, crushed
1/2 teaspoon thyme
2 bay leaves
1.5 litres water
Salt and pepper to taste

Place all the ingredients in a large soup pot. Bring to a boil, reduce the heat and simmer uncovered for 45 minutes. Strain and use immediately. Alternatively freeze or refrigerate until needed.

Curry too hot?

If your curry turns out to be too hot, add a carton of plain yoghurt or sour cream to take the edge off the heat.

Chilled wrap

Keep a roll of plastic wrap or cling film in the fridge as this makes it easy to find the end and unwrap.

Cleaning aluminium

To remove stains from an aluminium pan, fill it with water, add the juice of a lemon, and simmer gently until the metal brightens up.

Freezing minced meat

The freezing of minced beef (or any minced meat) can be made easier by following a few simple tips. First purchase good quality large plastic freezer bags. Place only 450 grams of minced meat in each bag and flatten the meat to a thin layer. Press to remove as much air as possible then seal the bag and freeze. This method allows for quick, safe freezing and for the meat to be thoroughly defrosted in the microwave oven without the usual browning around the edges.

12 'musts' for the kitchen cupboard

A well-stocked cupboard is the key to creating good meals in a hurry. Among the items you need to keep in the house are...

Stock (beef and chicken)
Milk powder
Dijon mustard
Olive oil
Canned diced tomatoes
Good quality spaghetti sauce

Cornflour
Rice
Sugar
Flour
Pasta
Onions

To this basic list add your own items to accommodate your family's individual tastes.

Cleaning enamel

To clean badly stained enamel pans, fill with a solution of two teaspoons bleach to a pint of water. Leave to soak for one hour and then rinse thoroughly.

Cleaning copper

To clean copper pans, make a thick paste of flour and vinegar. Use a kitchen cloth to rub over the copper until it is clean. Finally wash in hot water and dry.

Good quality cabbage

Before buying a cabbage, check that the heart is firm by pressing the centre with your thumb.

Reheating food

Cooked food, whether prepared at home or purchased, should not be reheated more than once. When food is reheated it should be heated until it is piping hot. Cooked food should not be kept warm, it should be kept piping hot or it should be cooled quickly and correctly stored – or eaten!

Opened cans

Empty the contents of a part used tin of food into a bowl, cover and refrigerate. Never store food in part emptied cans as the inside of the tin will begin to discolour and taint the food.

Safe storage

Always store raw meats and food to be defrosted beneath any cooked foods to avoid contamination from dripping juices. Leave foods wrapped unless their packaging recommends you do otherwise.

Salt substitution

To add to the flavour of most vegetables add a little fresh lemon juice instead of salt; this is most helpful to people on low salt diets.

Chilling bulk cooking

Foods that are prepared in large batches (soups and stews) are especially susceptible to harmful spoilage. It is always advisable to cool down the foods before placing them in the refrigerator. One way to do this is to add ice to your sink (with the plug in place). Place the pot of food on the ice and add water to the sink (about 3⁄4 of the way up the side of the pan). Stir the food frequently. When chilled cover and refrigerate. Another quick way to chill is to transfer the soup or stew to a shallow baking pan (like a lasagne dish) before refrigerating. This allows a faster, safer cool down.

Smelly flask?

To keep a vacuum flask fresh, add a teaspoon of white sugar to the clean dry empty flask before storing it. This will prevent stale smells from developing inside the closed flask.

Flour sieve

To evenly flour a work surface before working with pastry, sprinkle the flour through a sieve.

No matches?

If you have candles to light and no matches or lighter in your house, light one end of a long piece of dried spaghetti on the gas hob and use this as a taper.

Steaming asparagus

If you don't want to buy a special asparagus steamer, then use a deep saucepan and make a ring of baking foil to hold the asparagus heads out of the water so that they only steam while the bottoms boil in the water.

Dry marinating

'Dry rubs' are blends of ingredients (usually herbs, spices and salt) that are used to season meats just before grilling or smoking. For a fuller flavour allow the seasoned meats to marinate overnight in the refrigerator. Ensure that the product is covered with plastic wrap.

Saving scraps for stock

Stocks are the heart of great soups and sauces. Lots of items can be saved for stock making. Bag up carrot peels, onion skins, celery ends, parsley stems, and mushroom stems for use in preparing stocks. Other ingredients, from fish bones to chicken carcasses, can be frozen and contribute to a later stock.

Sharpening serrated knives

You should never sharpen serrated knives with a normal sharpening steel. When they are losing their 'edge' take them to a professional sharpener, unless you have a special sharpener for serrated knives.

Steaming without a steamer

To steam vegetables when you have not got a steamer use a metal sieve and a wide saucepan. Make sure that the sieve sits above the boiling water. Put the vegetables in the sieve and cover with a lid.

Skimming soups

When making soups it is a good idea to skim the fat and "foam" (impurities that rise to the top) during the early stages of cooking. Add any dried herbs after this process has been completed, as the herbs have a light texture and tend to also rise at this point, so if you've already added them they would be removed with the fat and impurities!

Easy-slice corned beef

Storing tinned corned beef in the fridge will make it much easier to slice when required.

Quick tomato and red pepper soup

1 can chopped tomatoes
1 red pepper – deseeded and roughly chopped
1 pint chicken or vegetable stock
A dash of cream for decoration (optional)

Put tomatoes into a saucepan and add the red pepper.
Then add the stock, bring to the boil and simmer for five
minutes. Finally liquidise until smooth and serve with a
swirl of cream if you want to be naughty!

Homemade peanut butter

Making homemade peanut butter is easy when using a
food processor. The following makes 1 jar...

3 1/2oz (100g) peanuts (shelled and unsalted)
1 1/2 tablespoons vegetable oil
Salt to taste

Pulse the peanuts in the processor until smooth (about
one minute). With the machine running, slowly add the
oil and run until smooth. Check the seasoning. Store
covered in the refrigerator.

What are crudités?

Easy additions to your party buffet are crudités – a
selection of raw vegetables. Cut celery, carrots, broccoli,
cauliflower or any other vegetable you enjoy into easy to
pick up and dip pieces. Arrange them decoratively on
a platter with your favourite dip or salad dressing. This
offers your guests a lighter choice than some of the higher
calorie items you may be offering later.

Green potatoes

Don't be overly concerned if your potato has a greenish
tinge on the skin. It is simply a chemical reaction caused
by exposure to light. It can, however, cause a bitter taste
so peel the potato before using. To prevent this occurring,
store potatoes away from any light source.

Tricky pouring!

Try lightly spraying your measuring jug with oil before
adding thick ingredients like treacle or honey. This will
help insure that the entire contents (and the correct
measurement) go into your recipe. It also makes cleanup
easier and reduces waste.

Need to use half an egg?

Although most recipes list the number of whole eggs to use, it can be useful to know a conversion measurement. This can come in handy if you want to make only half of a particular recipe. The average large egg is about 2oz (57g or 4 tablespoons). Simply lightly whip the egg and measure the required fraction.

Freezing herbs

Freezing rather than drying better preserves some herbs. You will sacrifice the fresh texture, but retain more of the flavour by freezing basil, chives, dill, parsley, and tarragon. Try to use frozen herbs within six months of harvesting.

Perfect thickening

When thickening with cornflour and water, always bring the food being cooked to a gentle boil before reducing the heat to a simmer. This will ensure that the thickener will reach its full degree of effectiveness.

What does 'butterfly' mean?

Sometimes you'll see the term 'butterfly' in a recipe. This means that the food item is split down the middle, without cutting it into two pieces. The end result is thought to resemble a butterfly. 'Butterflying' makes foods easier to stuff and can reduce cooking times.

Fragrant sugars

To make vanilla sugar, bury two vanilla pods in a jar
of sugar and leave for at least a week, shaking the jar
occasionally. In addition to vanilla pods, wonderfully
flavoured sugars can be produced by storing with lemon
zest, rose petals, or lavender.

No sour cream?

To make soured cream: add one teaspoon (5ml) of lemon
juice to 1/4 pint (150ml) of single cream, stir well and then
leave to thicken for 30 minutes.

Breading foods

Use this procedure to add flavour and to protect foods
when frying or sautéing....

Flour: Dredge the item to be cooked in plain or seasoned
flour. This will help the breading adhere to the food.

Egg wash: A basic mixture is 2 beaten eggs plus 1/2 cup
milk. Dip the floured item in the wash. Drain off any excess
before going to the next step. This will help bind the
breading and add moisture.

Crumbs: Breadcrumbs (dried or fresh) are commonly
used. Other items are sometimes used. Cover the food
well with the crumbs and gently press them in before
cooking.

Burnt-on food

To remove burnt-on food from a glass dish simply fill it
with hot water, drop in a denture cleaning tablet and leave
overnight. The next morning rinse well to leave a sparkling
dish!

Opening an oven

When opening oven doors, open the door a little at first, to allow the initial surge of heat and any steam from food being cooked to be released, and then open the door completely. Before opening it move your body away from the opening, and make sure you are not bent over with your head or any other part of your body directly above or near the opening.

Experiment with pesto

The ingredients in classic pesto (usually basil, olive oil, garlic, pine nuts and Parmesan) can be changed to create exciting new sauces. Different fresh herbs (or combinations) can be substituted. When using strong herbs (like tarragon or dill), try mixing them with equal parts of parsley. Walnuts are great in pesto. For a different flavour, try lightly toasting any nut used.

No corkscrew?

To uncork a bottle of wine without a corkscrew, screw a metal hook into the cork, put a wooden spoon handle through the hook, and pull the cork out. Cheers!

Accurate measuring

Proper measuring is essential when preparing food from a written recipe. Always assume that amounts are in "level" teaspoons or tablespoons unless otherwise stated.

Pureeing acid fruits

To puree acid fruits, such as raspberries, use a nylon sieve and a wooden spoon, as metal sieves and spoons may react with the acid in the fruit, and discolour the puree.

Buying stewing beef

Avoid the pre-cut diced 'stewing beef' in your supermarket's meat department. The pieces are usually end trimmings from various cuts and the price is often inflated. Your best bet is to buy a whole piece of beef and simply dice it yourself.

Special diets

Most recipes can be modified to accommodate special dietary needs. First isolate the ingredients that are undesirable. For example, someone on a low-fat diet would look for items like butter, eggs, milk, or cheese. These foods can be substituted with vegetable oil, eggbeaters, skimmed milk, and fat-free cheese. Remove chicken skin to reduce fat. Experiment with changing a high-fat cooking process (like frying) to sautéing or grilling.

Take good care of your chocolate

To maintain the quality of chocolate, store it wrapped
in a cool dry place. If it becomes too warm or damp,
some changes in flavour and texture may occur. Never
refrigerate fine chocolate. It is best to use chocolate within
six months of purchase – if it lasts that long!

Storing onions and garlic

Onions and garlic are best stored hung in strings so there is a good circulation of air to avoid disease spores causing mould. Most of us don't get time to do this properly these days so a great alternative is to put the onions or garlic in a nylon stocking, and tie a knot between each one to prevent them from touching. When you require an onion or garlic bulb then simply cut off just below a knot.

Food storage

Avoid keeping ingredients like herbs, oils, pastas and vinegars too near to the oven. The extreme heat can seriously alter the flavour of these delicate items. Also, never keep glass containers of any kind close to the heat of the cooker.

Buying fresh spinach

When purchasing fresh spinach look for dark green leaves with firm texture. Always wash spinach (even the pre-washed product). To store, dry the leaves using a spinner if possible, wrap in paper towels, place in a plastic food bag and refrigerate.

No shallots?

Shallots are an ingredient that many cooks don't always keep on hand. Using onions and garlic can make an acceptable substitute. For every tablespoon of shallots needed substitute a mix of 2/3 tablespoon of minced onion to 1/3 tablespoon of minced garlic.

Crystallized honey

If your runny honey isn't runny anymore but has begun to crystallize, stand the jar in a bowl of hot water for five minutes turning the jar a few times until the honey becomes clear and liquid.

Celery revival

To revive sticks of limp celery, place them in a bowl of ice-cold water for an hour. Adding a squeeze of fresh lemon to the water will greatly improve the flavour too.

Flakier pastry

When making flaky pastry, by substituting one teaspoon of cold water for one teaspoon of vinegar will give your pastry a much flakier crust.

Rescuing lumpy gravy

Lumpy gravy can be rescued! The usual cause is improper combining of liquid with roux (a mixture of flour and fat used to thicken). Simply strain the gravy through a fine mesh strainer or colander. Discard any lumps and continue to simmer the gravy until the desired thickness is reached.

Slicing bread

Improper slicing can ruin a beautiful homemade or bakery loaf of bread. Always slice fresh bread using a proper bread knife with a serrated blade. For best results remember to use a 'sawing' motion and press downward as little as possible. Let the knife do the work! Keep the top of the knife perpendicular to the loaf to ensure even slices. Always allow freshly-baked bread to cool on a rack before attempting to cut it.

Storing pesto

When storing pesto in your refrigerator, cover the surface
with a thin layer of olive oil and seal the container tightly.
This will keep the flavour fresh for several days and prevent
the product from darkening.

Chiffonade

If you come across the fancy term 'chiffonade' in a recipe
it simply means the method of cutting vegetables or herbs
into thin strips.

Pan sizes

This may sound obvious but always use tins and
saucepans of the right size when cooking! When roasting
make sure the roasting tin is large enough to hold the
food and any juices it may produce, thus preventing
fat from spitting over the sides or hot juices being spilt
when moving the tin. When cooking liquids make sure
the saucepan, casserole dish, or other container is large
enough so that boiling liquids do not splash or bubble
over, and again so it can be moved easily without spilling
the hot liquid.

Whipping cream

To create whipped cream with perfect texture, make sure the mixer bowl, beaters, and cream are well chilled. This also speeds up the time it takes to reach the 'firm peaks' stage. Be careful not to over-whip.

Separating eggs

To successfully separate an egg yolk from its white, carefully break the egg in half and tip the yolk carefully from one half shell to the other a number of times, letting the egg white fall into a bowl underneath as you do it. Alternatively, gently break the egg onto a saucer, place an egg-cup carefully over the yolk and whilst holding this firmly in place tip the egg white into a bowl, leaving the egg yolk under the egg cup. If a little egg yolk falls into the white whilst separating, use the eggshell as a scoop to collect it. The egg yolk is collected easily in this way, unlike trying to capture it with a spoon.

Storing tomatoes

Only store tomatoes in a fridge if they are ripe. You should not put under ripe tomatoes in the fridge as low temperatures spoil the ripening process.

Dry beans

Always soak dry beans before cooking them. It makes them more easily digestible. It also makes them cook more quickly. Cover the beans with cold water and allow them to soak overnight. Remember to change the water a few times and rinse the beans thoroughly before cooking. Alternatively you can use the "quick method" – bring to a boil, cook for 3 minutes, cover and allow to rest 1 hour. Finally there is a third possibility if you are in a hurry. Simply add the dry beans at the beginning of the recipe. You will have to allow for additional cooking time which can range from 30-60 minutes, depending on the type of bean.

Clogged garlic press

To clean out a clogged-up garlic press, use a toothbrush.
Preferably an old one!

Reviving cooked carrots

To add to the flavour of previously cooked carrots sprinkle a little orange juice over them just before reheating.

Cleaning processors and blenders

Some foods can get stuck in groves and seams when using a food processor or blender. These are possible places for harmful bacteria to grow. Cleaning the sharp blades is always a potential safety hazard. A quick way to clean these appliances is to let them clean themselves. Add warm water about 1/3 of the way up and add a dash of dishwashing liquid or 1/4 dishwashing tablet. Run the appliance until it is clean, rinse with warm water and allow to air dry.

Just enough marinade!

Some marinades are expensive to make. In order to prepare the correct amount, a simple formula can come in handy. In general, make 1/4 of a cup of marinade for every 1lb (450g) of meat. Frequent turning of the food can also stretch the marinade.

Frozen lemon

Slice fresh lemons, open freeze on a tray, then pack in the usual manner. Always there for that gin and tonic! Also try a slice of cucumber in gin and tonic instead of lemon. So refreshing!

Lighter batter

You can achieve a lighter batter when preparing foods by using liquids with carbonation instead of the water or milk stated in many recipes. Beer is great for full-flavoured foods because it also adds a little flavour of its own. Use it in batters for fish and onion rings. Foods like vegetable fritters are best when soda water replaces some of liquids in the batter.

Odour-free chopping board

After using a chopping board to prepare strong smelling foods, wash the board and then wipe over with a cut lemon. This will eliminate any odours.

No nutcracker?

To crack nuts without a nutcracker, use either a pair of
pliers or mole grips. With the nut held in place, wrap the
whole thing in a tea towel before you apply pressure,
which will avoid the bits going everywhere.

Choosing a pear

Pears are one of the only fruits that ripen better off the tree rather than on it. The best-tasting pears are those that are picked immature and allowed to ripen in storage or even on the grocer's shelf. Choose brightly coloured pears; avoid cut, shrivelled, or bruised pears, as they are likely to be bruised inside.

Storing mushrooms

Always store mushrooms in a paper bag at the bottom of the fridge.

Banish bacteria

Keep surfaces and equipment as clean as possible during the preparation of foods. Bacteria multiply rapidly in damp warm conditions, so a damp surface in the warmth of a kitchen is an ideal environment for them. There is also the benefit that the more cleaning that is done during the preparation process the less there is to be done at the end. Always wash and dry your hands thoroughly, with soap and hot water, before and after preparing food. This will help prevent the cross contamination of bacteria to the food that is being prepared.

Storing citrus

To store citrus fruits for longer than a week, wipe each fruit and wrap in newspaper. Pack into a polystyrene bag or box and store in a cool dry place.

Storing celery

Celery will keep for weeks in a fridge when wrapped in kitchen foil.

Lemon juice cubes

Like most fruit juices, lemon juice does not keep for very long before it loses its fresh taste in cooking. Fortunately, lemon juice can easily be frozen in ice cube trays so that it is always available when required. When a recipe calls for a tablespoon of lemon juice – just toss in a cube!

Odour-free hands

If you have been preparing fish, onion or garlic dishes and your hands smell to high Heaven, simply rub your hands over a stainless steel bowl, pan or other kitchen gadget – even the stainless steel taps – and the smell should disappear. Alternatively try washing your hands with lemon juice or dampening them and rubbing with salt before rinsing under running water.

Freezer labelling

Have you ever found a package of food in your freezer and asked yourself "What IS this?". You can avoid this dilemma simply by labelling each freezer bag with a permanent marker. Also remember that food does not keep indefinitely after freezing, so add the date of freezing to the label and check your frozen items at least once every month.

Yeast 'use by' dates

It is important to check the date of expiration on yeast
before adding it to a recipe. Yeast is a living ingredient and
won't perform correctly if it is past its prime. It is especially
important for the casual baker to check the date to avoid
wasting a lot of time and ingredients.

Useful substitutes

Breadcrumbs	Crushed cream crackers or cornflakes
Cornflour (1 tablespoon as a thickener)	2 level tablespoons plain flour
Single Cream (1/2 pint/285ml)	8fl.oz/225ml milk plus 2fl.oz/60ml melted unsalted butter
Honey (8fl.oz/225ml)	8oz/225g sugar plus 4 tablespoons water or golden syrup
Lemon juice (1 teaspoon)	1/2 teaspoon vinegar or lime juice
Ice Cream	Frozen yoghurt
Whole milk (1/2 pint/285ml)	1/2 pint/285ml skimmed milk plus 3 teaspoons melted butter
Noodles	Spaghetti
Tartare sauce	7 tablespoons mayonnaise plus 2 tablespoons chopped sweet mixed pickles
Tomato Sauce	Condensed tomato soup or a packet of tomato soup made up with half quantity of water
Gravy	Condensed tinned soup or packet soup made up with half the usual quantity of water

No self-raising flour?

If you are short of self-raising flour use plain flour with the addition of baking powder. The amount to add varies depending upon what is being cooked; however a usual amount would be 1 level teaspoon of baking powder to 4oz (113g) of flour.

Bitter almonds

The dark skin on whole almonds can sometimes add a bitter flavour. They might also make an undesirable visual presentation in some recipes. Simply add the almonds to a saucepan and cover with water. Bring to a boil, drain, and shock with cold water. Squeeze the almonds and most skins will come right off. Place the nuts on a baking sheet at 300°F /150°C /gas mark 2 for five minutes to crisp them back up.

Safe slicing

When slicing vegetables, use your knuckle to guide the knife and fold the finger tips back to prevent accidents.

Cracking a coconut

This is the most efficient way to crack a coconut: puncture one of its "eyes" with an ice pick or the tip of a sharp knife. Pour out the milk and save it. Then crack the coconut by hitting it with a hammer in the middle, where the shell is widest. Continue cracking around the nut until you have made a circle and can separate the two halves. Finally prise the coconut out of the shell. To shred it, remove the coconut flesh from the hard shell, along with the brown papery inner covering, and rub the coconut 'meat' against a food grater.

Chopsticks

Using chopsticks can be a fun way to break your daily dining routine. Many dieters find that they eat less because the pace of eating is slowed, especially when just learning to use them! The same slowing down of eating and ingesting smaller mouthfuls also aids digestion.

Keep vegetables green

When boiling green vegetables, keep the lid off the saucepan and they will stay greener!

Joint temperature

Make sure large joints of meat or poultry are cooked right through to the centre. A meat thermometer or probe is relatively inexpensive and can be used to check the final temperature in the centre of the item being cooked. Most harmful bacteria are killed when the temperature in the centre of the food reaches 160°F (70°C) for two or more minutes. As anyone who has ever experienced food poisoning will tell you – this is so worth doing!

Fresh herbs

Fresh herbs can add new levels of flavour to most recipes. Use two teaspoons of fresh, chopped herbs in place of one teaspoon of the dried equivalent. The flavour and intensity of most herb varieties are concentrated in the dehydration process.

Cooking perfect pasta

When cooking pasta it is not necessary to add oil to the water. The oil stays mainly on the surface and adds little to the taste. Cook the pasta in a pan of boiling, salted water. When cooked, drain and then pour extra virgin or virgin oil over and shake well. This will prevent the pasta from sticking together, and also give you all the flavour of the oil.

Greasy wrappers

Use the outer wrappers from packets of butter, lard etc. to grease and/or line baking tins.

Onions without tears

To stop your eyes shedding tears when chopping an onion make sure that the knife is razor sharp. If the knife is blunt it squeezes the moisture out when it gets to the cell walls, instead of cutting straight through them. The resulting liquid is what makes the tear ducts run.

Washing lettuce

Leafy lettuces should always be washed thoroughly before using. Fill a large bowl with cold water, separate the leaves and swirl them in the water. Allow them to sit in the bowl for a short time. If there is an excessive amount of dirt in the bottom of the bowl then repeat the process. Always dry the leaves before using, either in a salad spinner or by patting gently with a towel.

Mirrored service

For that important or special party, use a mirror tile from which to serve canapés instead of a plate. These can be bought relatively cheaply from a DIY store.

Frozen herbs

If you have a glut of fresh herbs here's a great way to store them... Take an ice cube tray, finely chop the fresh herbs and place some into each section of the tray. Add a little fresh water to each section and then freeze. Remove the frozen cubes of herbs and add to recipes as required.

Soup for sauce

Use condensed soup as a quick and easy sauce. A great example is to cut some leftover chicken into cubes and mix with either condensed chicken or mushroom soup and serve on a bed of rice. "Chicken a la King" in minutes!

Freezing bread

When freezing sliced bread place greaseproof between the slices so that you can remove just the number of slices you need without having to thaw the whole loaf.

Pastry mix

Save precious time by mixing your pastry to the 'breadcrumb' stage (i.e. rubbing in the flour and fat), and then put this mixture into an airtight container in the freezer. It is a good idea to make quite a large amount. When you want to make pastry, take out enough of the dry mixture for your requirements and add the water in the usual way (1 teaspoon of water for every 25 grams of mixture). This mixture can also be used to make crumble by just adding sugar.

Blow-dried jar

To dry a tall spaghetti jar quickly after washing, use a hair dryer!

Quick jackets

For a better textured baked potato than those that you microwave try this method for speeding up the potato baking process. Pre-heat the oven to 400°F/200°C/gas mark 6. Place the potato in boiling water for 10 minutes, and then bake for 30 minutes. This will cut the cooking time in half.

Care with spices

Don't measure or shake spices over open boiling saucepans, as you may drop too much into the pan. Also the steam might enter the jar, causing the spice grains to stick together in lumps and therefore spoil.

Making chopped tomatoes

Canned chopped tomatoes are more expensive than whole ones. Save money by buying cans of whole ones and chopping them up, whilst still in the can, with a pair of scissors.

Freezer rules

- Do not refreeze food after it has been thawed.

- Thawed raw food can be frozen after it has been cooked.

- Thawed cooked food should not be refrozen.

- Check the contents of the freezer every so often to make sure that storage times for the particular foods are not exceeded.

- Always buy frozen foods as the last thing when shopping and take them straight to the freezer when you get home. Wrapping frozen items together, and placing them in an insulated bag or box, will help to prevent their temperature from rising.

- Food is best thawed placed in or on a suitable container in the fridge. Do not thaw items by placing them in hot or warm water as it will be difficult to determine if the centre has thawed properly, particularly with large joints of meat or poultry.

Piping hot is perfect!

Ovens and appliances can vary in their accuracy and efficiency, so always check that food is piping hot right through to the centre before serving. Even if you are following a recipe or instructions on the packaging of frozen foods, check to make sure that it is thoroughly cooked.

Storing foods

Cooked and fresh foods should not be stored in the same container. They should be packaged and stored separately. This will avoid cross contamination between stored items. Do not put warm food in the fridge, make sure it has been cooled correctly and quickly. This will avoid unnecessary changes in temperature and the formation of condensation, which can easily affect other items being stored as well as the efficiency of the fridge.

Storing hard cheese

Keep hard cheeses such as mature Cheddar or Parmesan moist during storage by wrapping in a clean piece of cloth that has been dampened with beer. Keep in an airtight container in a refrigerator for one to two weeks.

Sauces

This first sauce is the basis of most white sauces, both sweet and savoury. Follow the recipes to the letter and you will never have lumpy sauces again!

Béchamel sauce

1 pint (600ml) milk, 1 onion with 2 cloves stuck in, 1 carrot (peeled and chopped), bouquet garni, 1¾oz (50g) butter, 1¾oz (50g) flour, salt, freshly ground black pepper, freshly grated nutmeg.

Into a saucepan put the milk, onion, carrot and bouquet garni. Bring slowly to the boil and then reduce the heat to a slow simmer for 30 minutes to infuse. In a separate saucepan melt the butter and stir in the flour with a wooden spoon. This is called making a 'roux'. Cook for about one minute stirring constantly – this is very important otherwise the finished sauce will have a floury taste. Remove the saucepan from the heat and gradually add the milk a little at a time. Stir vigorously all the time. At this stage the sauce should be runny without any lumps. Return the pan to the heat and simmer gently for about five minutes until the sauce thickens.

Variations: Add tarragon, parsley etc. to make different sauces.

Tomato sauce

2 tablespoons olive oil, 1 medium onion (finely chopped),
2 crushed cloves garlic, 2fl.oz (60ml) red wine, 1¾lb
(800g) tinned tomatoes, 2 tablespoons tomato ketchup, ½
tablespoon dried thyme, ½ tablespoon dried basil.

Heat the oil in a saucepan, add onion and garlic and cook
until soft but not coloured. Add the wine and simmer
until reduced by half. Add the rest of the ingredients and
simmer for 10 minutes or until thickened. This recipe can
be frozen for storage.

Basic cheese sauce

1¾oz (50g) butter, 1¾oz (50g) flour, 13fl.oz (400ml) milk,
1½oz (40g) mature Cheddar cheese.

Put the milk into a saucepan, bring slowly to the boil and
then reduce the heat to a slow simmer. In a separate
saucepan melt the butter and stir in the flour with a
wooden spoon. This is called making a 'roux'. Cook for
about a minute, stirring constantly – this is very important
otherwise the finished sauce will have a floury taste.
Remove the saucepan from the heat and gradually add
the milk, a little at a time. Stir vigorously all the time. At
this stage the sauce should be runny without any lumps.
Return the pan to the heat and simmer gently for about five
minutes until the sauce thickens. Remove from the heat,
allow to cool very slightly, and then stir in the cheese.

Velouté sauce

1¾oz (50g) butter, 1¾oz (50g) flour, 16fl.oz (500ml) chicken stock, 1 bay leaf, 2 sprigs parsley, 1 sprig thyme, 6 black peppercorns.

In a saucepan melt the butter, stir in the flour and heat for about a minute stirring continuously. Remove the saucepan from the heat and gradually add the stock, stirring all the time. Add the remainder of the ingredients, and return the pan to the heat. Simmer gently for about 25 minutes. Skim any fat from the surface of the sauce during the cooking. Strain sauce through a fine sieve.

Variation: Add a little double cream after the sieving stage for an even richer sauce.

Vinaigrette

6 tablespoons virgin olive oil, 2 tablespoons white wine vinegar, 1 teaspoon dark smooth Dijon mustard, pinch sugar, salt and pepper.

In a glass bowl whisk together the oil and vinegar with a small balloon whisk. Whisk in the mustard and sugar until mixed thoroughly. Add salt and pepper to taste.

Mint sauce

4fl.oz (125ml) water, 2½oz (75g) sugar, 8fl.oz (250ml) cider vinegar, handful chopped mint.

In a small saucepan heat the water until hot but not boiling, add the sugar and stir to dissolve. Now bring to the boil and boil rapidly for five minutes. Remove from the heat, stir in the vinegar and mint, and leave to stand for 10-15 minutes. Stir before serving.

Creamy tarragon and mushroom sauce

1oz (28g) butter, 9oz (250g) sliced mushrooms, 2fl. oz (60ml) dry white wine, 1 tablespoon brandy, ½ pint (300ml) double cream, 2 teaspoons water, 1 teaspoon arrowroot, 1 tablespoon chopped chives, 1 teaspoon tarragon.

In a saucepan melt the butter, then add the mushrooms and stir gently until soft. Add the wine and brandy and simmer gently for about five minutes. In a cup mix together the water and arrowroot and add this to the pan. When the sauce thickens stir in the herbs.

A great sauce to accompany pasta, beef or pork!

Shopping with children

When you can't avoid taking the children along shopping for food, try incorporating them in the task. Divide up your list and let the youngsters help find the items for you. For little ones who already know how to count it can be an experience in counting or a form of language development and learning, as they discover the names of their favourites food.

Christmas tips

Christmas is a most wonderful time of year. Family and friends meet to celebrate, and everything seems to buzz with excitement as festivities fill the air. The atmosphere should be one of happiness and giving. However, so often as Christmas approaches, panic surrounds us as we worry about how to entertain, what to serve, how much to cook, and so on. Here are a few tips to ease the anxiety....

- The holiday spreads over several days and even into New Year, so careful planning is essential. If possible, plan for each day of this hectic period. Consider which foods will be left over (such as poultry and produce), and select recipes using these ingredients. Freeze food for unexpected arrivals.

- Make a fish and meat pâté, and freeze whole, or slice first (to thaw more quickly later). Served with a salad and crusty bread, a pâté makes a delicious, impromptu meal.

- Freeze a few puddings or gateaux for impressive desserts. Frozen finger foods also make marvellous standbys and certainly take the pressure out of entertaining at short notice, so prepare a tasty selection of these tempting, bite-size foods to serve with drinks.

Continued over the page...

Christmas tips continued...

- Once you have planned menus and calculated how many visitors are expected, determine which recipes can be made in advance and frozen or stored until required, such as Christmas cakes, puddings, and mince pies. Make detailed lists of food to be purchased in advance and at the last minute. Several weeks beforehand, stock up on drinks and easily-stored ingredients for nibbles, avoiding the rush in the days leading up to Christmas.

- Edible gifts, such as preserves, brandied mincemeat, fruits in liqueurs, pretty sweets, and cookies are most attractive in baskets, boxes, or dainty glass or china dishes. Assorted cheeses make a nice last-minute present and look especially good in a basket with crackers, butter, and an attractive, festive napkin. Cookies or gingerbread houses serve as perfect novelty gifts for children. A mini-Christmas cake with a few mince pies is a most welcome offering for someone living alone, or make up a mini-hamper of homemade goodies, such as pâté, preserves, cake, Christmas pudding, and cookies.

So with good planning and thinking ahead we can take the stress out of Christmas! Now that you feel happier about the whole occasion, vow to get off to the best possible start by making lists of all the things you will need to do under different headings such as:

Jobs to do	e.g. tidy and clear fridge, freezer, cupboards, shelves etc.
General food shopping	e.g. flour, sugar etc.
General non-food shopping	e.g. turkey size foil, cling film etc.
Week before Christmas	e.g. eggs, bacon, frozen pastry.
Last few days before Christmas	e.g. potatoes, vegetables, fruit, bread etc.

Christmas day vegetables

Prepare vegetables like carrots, parsnips, Brussels sprouts etc. on Christmas Eve and store them in the refrigerator in sealed plastic bags.

To make serving easier, cook the vegetables a couple of hours earlier than you need them for the meal. When they are almost ready, drain them – keeping the water to make the gravy – then plunge the vegetables into cold water to stop the cooking process.

Place them into serving dishes, and microwave to reheat at the last moment.

Turkey

Now let's tackle the turkey! If you are going to buy a frozen turkey then buy it at the beginning of December when the shops are quiet. You need to allow 12oz (300g) of meat per person. When you get the turkey home, make a note somewhere in the kitchen of when you need to take the turkey out of the freezer. The importance of this cannot be over emphasised! As well as the recommended thawing time you need to allow an extra 8-10 hours. The idea is to get the bird completely thawed out by Christmas Eve. You then need to place the turkey in a very cool room, such as a spare room with the radiator off, to bring it back to room temperature before cooking.

- For thawing in a fridge at 4°C, allow 12 hours per 2.2lb (1kg); so 4 days for a 17½lb (8kg) turkey.

- For thawing in a cool room at 15°C, allow 7 hours per 2.2lb (1kg); so 56 hours for a 17½lb (8kg) turkey.

- For thawing at room temperature at 20°C, allow 2 hours per 2.2lb (1kg); so 16 hours for an 17½lb (8kg) turkey.

Obviously your fridge or room may have a different temperature from those listed so you may need to allow more or less time than quoted.

A few tips for a perfect roast turkey!

Cooking the stuffing in the turkey cavity is not recommended as it takes longer to cook the turkey, and it is also more difficult to make sure that the turkey is cooked through properly. It is acceptable (and very pleasant!) to use the cavity to tuck a bunch of herbs, a lemon, or a whole onion inside the carcass of a turkey before roasting. The flavour will penetrate the meat, and will make tasty juices for the gravy.

* Keep the breast of birds such as turkey, pheasant or pigeon moist and tender by laying bacon rind or streaky bacon over the breast before roasting.

Continued over the page...

More turkey tips....

- Before placing the turkey in a roasting tin, cover the base of the tin with celery sticks. These will act like a roasting rack and will add flavour to the meat juices to make a most delicious gravy.

- Instead of covering a large turkey with foil for roasting, dip a double layer of muslin into melted butter or oil, and lay it over the bird's skin. The muslin will allow the skin to brown and become crisp during cooking without trapping in steam as a covering of foil would do.

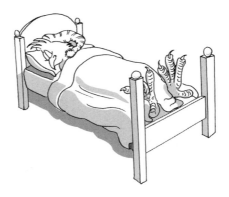

- Allow poultry to rest for about 20 minutes after roasting. This will make it easy to carve. Turn off the oven and leave the bird inside or remove and cover with foil.

- Cooking poultry in a roasting bag will eliminate the need for basting. If you want to crisp up the skin, open the bag for the final 20 minutes of cooking time.

And finally....

Even when most of the meat has been removed from your turkey, don't throw away the bones. Break up the carcass and place the pieces in a large pot. Cover with water. Add chopped onions, celery, carrots, and parsley to the pan. Simmer for a few hours and strain. Use this stock to make soups, gravy, and sauces. If, by now, you are a little tired of turkey, simply freeze it for later use when you want to re-live the flavours of Christmas!

Conversion tables and cooking times

Weight conversions

To convert...	Multiply by....
Grams to ounces	0.0353
Grams to pounds	0.0022
Kilograms to pounds	2.2046
Kilograms to tons	0.00098
Tonnes to tons	0.9842
Ounces to grams	28.35
Pounds to grams	453.592
Pounds to kilograms	0.4536
Tons to kilograms	1016.05
Tons to tonnes	1.016

Liquid conversions (approximate) - imperial, metric and US

Imperial	Metric	US Cups
1/2 fl oz	15 ml	1 level tablespoon
1 fl oz	30 ml	1/8 cup
2 fl oz	60 ml	1/4 cup
3 fl oz	90 ml	3/8 cup
4 fl oz	125 ml	1/2 cup
5 fl oz - 1/4 pint	150 ml	2/3 cup
6 fl oz	175 ml	3/4 cup
8 fl oz	250 ml	1 cup
10 fl oz - 1/2 pint	300 ml	1 1/4 cups
12 fl oz	375 ml	1 1/2 cups
16 fl oz	500 ml	2 cups - 1 US pint
20 fl oz - 1 pint	600 ml	2 1/2 cups
1 1/2 pints	900 ml	3 3/4 cups
1 3/4 pints	1 litre	4 cups - 1 quart
2 pints	1 1/4 litres	1 1/4 quarts
2 1/3 pints	1 1/2 litres	3 US pints
3 1/4 pints	2 litres	2 quarts

Handy kitchen measures

The following are equivalent to
approximately 1oz or 28g:

1 level tablespoon	Salt
3 level tablespoons	Flour
2 level tablespoons	Rice
5 level tablespoons	Grated cheese
4 level tablespoons	Cocoa powder
1 level tablespoon	Honey/syrup/jam
2 level tablespoons	Granulated sugar
3 level tablespoons	Sifted icing sugar
6 level tablespoons	Fresh breadcrumbs
4 level tablespoons	Porridge oats

Spoon measures

1 tablespoon (tblsp)	3 teaspoons
1 level tablespoon (tblsp)	15ml
1 level teaspoon (tsp)	5ml

- A tablespoon or tblsp., when referring to dry goods (i.e. flour etc.), usually means a rounded tablespoon.

- A rounded tablespoon means there is as much of the product you are measuring above the top edge of the spoon as there is in the 'bowl' of the spoon.

- A heaped tablespoon means as much as you can get onto the spoon without it falling off.

- A level tablespoon is where the ingredient is level only with the top edge of the spoon. To achieve this, fill the spoon and then run a knife horizontally across the top, discarding anything above the level of the spoon. Of course, do make sure you have something underneath to catch it!

- A stick of butter is equal to half a cup, 4 oz, 8 tablespoon or 113 grams.

Oven temperatures

Degrees Fahrenheit (°F)	Degrees Celsius (°C)	Gas mark	Description
225	110	1/4	Very slow
250	120/130	1/2	Very slow
275	140	1	Slow
300	150	2	Slow
325	160/170	3	Moderate
350	180	4	Moderate
375	190	5	Moderately hot
400	200	6	Moderately hot
425	220	7	Hot
450	230	8	Hot
475	240	9	Very Hot

Cooking times

Approximate cooking times are shown in the tables to follow. Different appliances may vary in their efficiency and cooking times are also affected by the position of shelves in the oven. Always make sure food is properly cooked before serving. A meat thermometer or probe can be used to check the final temperature in the centre of a joint or item being cooked. If using a fan-assisted oven refer to the manufacturer's user manual for the necessary cooking adjustment. As a guide, lower the oven temperature by 40°F / 20°C, or the cooking times by 15 per cent.

Roast chicken

Cooked in the centre of the oven at 375°F/190°C/gas mark 5, 20 mins per 1lb (450g) + 20 mins. When neck end is stuffed allow an extra five minutes per 1lb (450g).

- Test that it's cooked by pressing a skewer into the deepest part of each thigh; the juices released should be clear and not contain any blood.

- For carving, remove the chicken from the oven and allow it to rest for approximately five minutes. This allows the meat to set, making carving easier.

Roast meats

Cooked in the centre of the oven at 350°F/180°C/gas mark 4 to 375°F/190°C/gas mark 5.

Meat	Rare	Medium	Well done
Beef	20 mins per 1lb (450g) +20 mins	25 mins per 1lb (450g) + 25 mins	30 mins per 1lb (450g) + 30 mins
Lamb	X	25 mins per 1lb (450g) + 25 mins	30 mins per 1lb (450g) + 30 mins
Pork	X	30 mins per 1lb (450g) + 30 mins	35 mins per 1lb (450g) + 35 mins

- To check the meat is cooked, place on a tray and press firmly to make sure the juices released are clear and do not contain any blood.

- In general all meats should be cooked through.

- Pork must always be cooked thoroughly.

- Lamb may be served pink, but must be cooked through.

- Beef is normally served slightly underdone and a little blood should show in the juice.

- For carving, remove the joint from the oven and allow it to rest for approximately 10 minutes. This allows the meat to set, making carving easier, and reducing the tendency for the meat to shrink and curl.

Roast turkey

Cooked in the centre of the oven at 375°F/190°C/gas mark 5.

If wrapped in foil increase the overall cooking time by 15 minutes, removing the foil for the last 30 minutes to allow the skin to brown.

If you stuff the turkey add the weight of the stuffing to calculate the total weight.

Oven ready weight	Total cooking time
6-7lb (2.5-3kg)	2 1/4 - 21/2 hours
8-9lb (3.5-4kg)	2 1/2 - 3 hours
10-11lb (4.5-5kg)	3 - 3 1/2 hours
12-13lb (5.5-6kg)	3 1/4 - 3 1/2 hours
14-17lb - (6.5-7kg)	3 1/2 - 3 3/4 hours
18-22lb (8-10kg)	3 3/4 - 4 1/4 hours
23lb plus (10.5kg plus)	4 1/4 hours plus

• Test that it's cooked by pressing a skewer into the deepest part of each thigh; the juices released should be clear and not contain any blood.

• For carving, remove the turkey from the oven and allow it to rest for approximately 10-15 minutes. This allows the meat to set, making carving easier.

Fish

Whole fish	Grill (mins)	Fry (mins)	Micro-wave (mins) 750 watts	Steam (mins)	Bake (mins)	Poach (mins)
Plaice (300g)	13	5	3-4	20	15-18	5-6
Lemon sole (500g)	13	12	4-5	20	20	9
Dover sole (500g)	9	9	4-5	20	20	5
Dabs (400g)	9	9	3-4	20	20	4
Mackerel (300g)	15	15	3-4		25	
Sea Bass (400g)	18	15	3-4	22	30	
Sea bream	18	15	3-4	22	30	
Fillets (200g)						
Cod	17	5	3-4	15	18	5
Whiting	9	5	1-2	10-12	9	3-4
Lemon Sole	9	4	1-2	10-12	9	3-4
Plaice	9	5	1-2	10-12	9	3-4
Turbot	9	6	2-3	10-12	12	5-8
Steaks (to cook one steak)						
Cod	10	8-10	4-5	10-15	20-25	10

Index

Notes

Notes

Notes

Notes

Notes

Notes

'The Greatest Tips In The World'

'The Greatest Tips In The World' is a unique series of fun and informative hints and tips books, devised and created by Steve Brookes and written by authors who are experts in their field.

This fabulous collection of books will grow each year to cover many home and leisure interests with Gardening Tips, Golfing Tips, DIY Tips, Cookery Tips and Household Tips being the first five titles in the series. With many more to follow, these books will form a most useful compilation for any bookshelf!

For more information about currently available books, forthcoming titles and the authors, please visit:

www.thegreatestintheworld.com

or write to:

Public Eye Publications
PO Box 3182
Stratford-upon-Avon
Warwickshire CV37 7XW

The Author

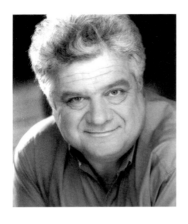

Peter Osborne, 'The Big Chef', is one of the most accomplished cookery presenters around with an exceptional ability to communicate his passion for cooking in a lively and fun way. For the past 5 years he has performed his live cookery show all over Britain and Europe.

Peter's TV credits include Granada TV, Breeze & Carlton Food Network, BBC Breakfast and This Morning, as well as air time on European and USA networks. He has a regular cookery spot on 'The Graham Rogers Show' at Classic Gold Radio.

In addition to broadcast work Peter regularly contributes to a variety of publications where his recipes and columns entertain and inform with his frank yet witty trademark style. He also has published two books 'Happy Cooking' and 'Simply Scrumptious'. You can find out more about 'The Big Chef' by visiting his website at www.thebigchef.com.